# THE TALE OF A CANDID TWEEN

## TOLD THROUGH 25 POEMS

## ANIKA MALHOTRA

To my generation that struggles to understand itself

and

To the people who try to understand us

# Contents

# Contents

# Foreword

Very rarely do I come across a young tween who has such a profound thought process that early in her life. Anika Malhotra might be an 11-year-old tween at the cusp of teenhood, but the way she writes, imagines, and expresses her thoughts, angst, dilemmas and experiences through poetry is quite commendable.

She is no longer a kid, and she announces *how* in her maiden poetry collection.

She skillfully demonstrates her ability to write open verse with excellent command over her language, much beyond her age or experience.

Through this collection of poems, she talks about her experiences in the last two years of lost childhood during the pandemic. Having woven a world of her own through these emotions, she has illustrated unique, weird, confusing, disappointing and ecstatic moments from her life.

My best wishes to her for her poetry collection, and I am sure that her peers and adults will find her expression relevant, and her words will resonate with all.

Dr. Dwarika Uniyal

Noted Academic, Author, Poet and Entrepreneur

# Preface

Unapologetic - that's what comes to mind when I am asked to describe my age group, the *in-betweeners* that aren't officially teens yet.

Though tweens are quite young, they are an oft-forgotten generation. Adults assume they understand our sentiments, and they go about their heydays, categorizing our personalities and conducting workshops to figure us out. At the same time, we tweens twiddle our thumbs, trying to find our ideal personality types.

I don't blame them. Due to many emotions and personalities running loose, nobody understands a word that tweens say. Even I don't understand myself.

I want to make sure that everyone knows about the challenges and hardships that all tweens go through. To let people better understand a tween's life, I have written this compilation of poems in an unrestrained, raw voice that candidly speaks to all.

No sudden personalities. No secrets, I promise you.

# Acknowledgements

I know this might sound cliché, but I would like to thank my parents. I'm extremely thankful that they supported me through everything I have wanted to do and always looked out for me.

Secondly, I would like to thank my friends - only a few of them, though (you know who you are) for helping me maintain my happiness throughout the darkest of times.

And lastly, I want to thank Mr Bijit Sinha. I met him first in fourth grade, and since then, he has never stopped encouraging me in my writing pursuits.

# 1. Almost Eleven

*Walking the living room*
*The room is so empty yet so full*
*I have a pint of ice cream in my hands*
*everyone wants some*
*They take it and make no conversation*
*It's like I'm not even there*
*I want to go away, yet they want me here*
*I'll just watch a movie*
*"Get an adult"*
*I say "never mind"*
*15 minutes & everyone cares*
*now it's gone*
*"I'll go talk to my friends"*
*everyone is so much louder;*
*no one noticed I was gone*
*It's almost like it's not even my birthday*

# 2. A Short Life

"*Life is short, live it out*"
*I mean I would, if a virus wasn't at my snout*
*I'd be out all day riding my bike*
*except life hits me with challenges throughout*
*I could be watching tv all day*
*but then I get a homework assignment*
*That's just fine; I'll read a book*
*- educational yet fun*
*(is this supposed to be a loophole?)*
*Though getting older is fun*
*I hope these years quickly pass*
*Maybe then life won't feel like one long class*

# 3. Never-ending Journey

*When you are young, they assume you know nothing*
*each day accomplishes thousands of things*
*maybe you did some of them*
*but they still think you are a bystander*
*Maybe you're just not old enough…*


*The older you get, the smarter you are*
*but they won't believe you unless you know pi by heart;*
*they won't believe you until you find the cure to cancer;*
*your accomplishments mean nothing until you break all odds -*
*to them, that is the case*

# 4. Early Life Cycle

*Wake up*

*eat*

*go to sleep -*

*whatever happens in between*

*is forgotten in a week*

*Sometimes it's traumatizing*

*Sometimes it's sad*

*Maybe even a mix of the good and bad*

*At the end of the day*

*it's an endless cycle.*

*There's no fast way to end it*

*unless you're suicidal*

*It's either that or we keep living*

*It's okay for a while*

*but then you think*

*"This is so pointless"*

*and because of that, you are much wiser*

# 5. Ways to be Alone

*Video games all day:*
*"you're wasting too much time"*
*laughing so much that you might break your spine:*
*"what's so funny?"*
*it's almost like "living my life" is a mistake*
*everything you do is wrong*
*"do something right for once"*
*the last time I checked, life doesn't have an instruction manual*
*if it did, I'd be its first buyer*
*~to not get corrected each time~*
*if only I wasn't in the midst of it all*
*the answer isn't always there*
*sometimes time is the best answer*
*Just do your thing,*
*then everyone goes away*
*and you can finally be alone*

# 6. Leveling Up

*Fighting about the stupidest things*
*because problems 'aren't real' at this age;*
*sometimes life sucks no matter what phase you're on*
*- almost like a video game -*
*the higher the level, the harder it gets*
*but the better you become;*
*when the game ends you have nothing left*
*no proof to show*
*Use this logic in real life*
*What did you do?*
*How will anyone know you ever existed?*
*Won't you leave your mark?*

# 7. Emotions Bottled-up

*Emotions exist*
*whether you believe it or not;*
*crying doesn't make you 'soft'*
*it doesn't make you 'a girl'.*
*Emotions are shown in any way possible*
*trying to fix what can't be un-done.*
*Emotional is a funny word*
*it's only used when you show 'too much emotion to everyone'*
*But really, what is 'too much emotion?'*
*talking about your day being bad? (that can't be it)*
*being sad because you failed a test? (that's not too much)*
*someone you know is dying? (that's sad but I don't see how that's*
*'oversharing')*
*some terms were created by old English men describing women or*
*children*
*but really, there are some words to be thought of, not spoken*
*some things to say, not keep them in*
*some tears to shed, not bottle them up*
*some words to scream, not write them down*
*Emotions exist.*
*Better learn to tolerate them*
*or better yet: be authentic and stand up for yourself*

# 8. Think Before You...

*Can't do anything*
*without being compared*
*Can't say a word*
*without being prepared*
*You've got to think twice*
*before you do anything*
*The wrong kind could end you in a second -*
*make tears flow like you've never cried before*
*make you think your life was a mistake*
*Do anything the wrong way*
*and you're gone forever*
*Make your happiness as light as a feather;*
*so before you talk*
*think twice.*
*Though it's not necessary*
*it's a guide on how to survive*

# 9. The Kind of Pain that Matters

*Only visible pain exists*
*it's like mental health was never there*
*"oh, you're depressed?"*

*Well, they won't care*
*unless you have scars all over your hands*
*"what doesn't kill you makes you stronger"*

*It really just gives you PTSD*
*No one will care*
*You will always have to be there*
*no matter what*
*If it's not a 'real problem'*
*in their eyes*
*it will never matter*

# 10. Respect Your Elders

*Respect your elders*
*no matter what*
*If they shout at you, it's your fault*
*If they hurt you, they're just disciplining you*
*No matter what*
*it is your fault*
*It's because you didn't take care of yourself well*
*No matter what, it leads back to you*
*"so what if you got hurt?*
*deal with it"*
*Pain isn't real unless they can see it*

# 11. Why You're Wrong

*Everyone can think up reasons about why you are wrong*
*But when you are right, they won't care at all*
*Only looking at flaws*
*Crying at night*
*out of their sight*
*because you are trying to be strong*
*Hiding your pain*
*after them being vain*
*While knowing that you're right*
*and not putting up a fight*
*all because you know the ways of 'a kid'*

# 12. Safe Space

*On my computer all day*
*because technology is my safe space*
*No one can hate me*
*and everyone is nice*
*I have people with my sense of humor*
*and everything is right*
*The real world is great*
*I'm not saying it isn't*
*But telling me to 'get off my phone'*
*While you're on yours*
*really makes no sense*
*Praise what you preach*
*Understand that*
*I only connect online,*
*when I get to hide my face*

# 13. Family Reunions

*If you're not in the pictures, then you weren't there*
*If there is no one to remember that you were there*
*then were you really there?*
*they won't let you talk to anyone*
*they won't let you go away*
*they want you there*
*Yet they don't acknowledge you*
*you get on your device*
*you get tired*
*And right when the clock strikes 12*
*they shout at you*
*saying you didn't 'talk enough'*

# 14. Faces I Wear

*I wear a fake face*
*all day and night*
*no one sees me sad*
*no one sees me scared*
*Everyone sees me as 'a happy little child'*
*the only time I take it off*
*is in the corner of my room*
*When I come out*
*I'm happy again*
*because all the sadness is gone*

# 15. Compliment Days

*"I am impressed"*
*Those are words you barely hear*
*You only hear them when you're learning how to walk*
*No one speaks of a compliment, after you turn 10*
*Because after then, the only thing*
*that will get a compliment*
*is if you're becoming a doctor*
*Because that is apparently the only thing*
*that gets a smile out of them*

# 16. Undying Dreams

*"Get on the stage, it's your turn now"*
*I feel sick to my stomach*
*thinking about what could go wrong*
*~trembling in fear~*
*~shivering inside~*
*~hands are shaking~*
*But no one cares*
*"It's for publicity"*
*and though it might scare*
*I am well aware*
*But the trembles never leave my skin*
*they never go away*
*they are here to stay*
*So I shall listen*
*and faithfully fulfill the undying dreams*
*that were once placed on my seniors*

# 17. The Right Kind of Hobbies

*Join me in a match*

*hop in a VC*

*just me and my friends*

*life is so easy*

*If I could stay in this moment forever*

*I would*

*But at some point, they might want to come and force me to read*

*a book*

*or a pastime that I cannot connect with*

*If happiness was a real thing*

*I could freeze time*

*and stay in my happy place, forever and always*

# 18. Four Levels of Life

*-life has levels*
*complete them one by one-*
*Level 1 –*
*Child: everything is great, everyone is friends*
*and school is fun and games; no one can be rude*
*because you're just 'a kid'*

*Level 2 –*
*Tween: your body is changing, you're learning more,*
*you're discovering your personality, and school is a big bore*
*everyone is ignoring you because you either talk too much or too*
*little*

*Level 3 –*
*Adult: though I can't talk about this from my own point-of-view*
*I'd like to believe that it'll be better; the stakes are high and so is*
*your stress*
*and everyone expects you to be in a little white dress*
*Level 4 –*
*Senior Citizen: though your days left are very few, everyone does*
*love you*
*You are old and very likeable now*

*Though everyone spends time with you*
*you know it's for your will*
*Though some might truly love you, I guess we'll never know*
*The only time you find out is when you go*

# 19. School Routine

*7' o'clock -*
*wake up on the dot*
*go to school*
*learn a lot*
*They say it helps*
*Maybe it does*
*But what does it teach*
*other than textbook stuff?*
*They don't teach me how to feel*
*They don't teach me to see the world for what it is*
**Behave**
**Tow in line**
**Pay attention**
*: a murmured yes to all*
*We could be helping the world*
*But for today, a 'yes, ma'am/sir' is what fetches a reward*
*School is a selective place*
*~survival of the finest~*
*The other ones stay scarred*
*though at the end*
*everyone believes it magically works out.*

# 20. What's Right and What's Wrong

*"Learn from your mistakes"*
*Though it's overused*
*there is a 50/50 chance*
*that it's absolutely true*
*Though you only hear it from family and teachers*
*it helps in the real world*
*A mistake I made was 'not thinking before I speak'*
*After that day, my conversations were bleak*
*It's not learning if it's forced*
*"shut your mouth"*
*After that, I stopped talking*
*One more word, and maybe I'll stop walking*
*If there are still ways that I am wrong*
*Then what really defines right or wrong?*

# 21. How to be Normal

*-abnormal-*
*That's what they say I am*
*But really, what does that word mean?*
*It means not fitting the boundaries of 'normal'*
*But who knows what's normal and what isn't?*
*If only there were a rulebook prescribed for this*
*like the ones we've always been instructed to follow*
*telling the world what's good and bad*
*some gainly advice that could make life a bit less sad*
*Difficulty level of life would go down to Medium*
*- though you would feel manufactured -*
*But isn't that a worthy sacrifice to be the very 'best'?*

# 22. What Makes a Tween

*Being a tween isn't different*
*or the same as being a kid*
*It doesn't carry the fulfillment*
*I once thought it would*
*It's actually kind of 'boring'*
*- that is an emotion, last I checked -*
*Though that may be 'cause of Covid*
*Inside my mind, I'm snoring*
*Because there is no change in circumstances*
*In short, what I mean to say*
*is that no matter what you do or think*
*age doesn't matter anyway*
*unless of course, you want a drink*
*With this new stage,*
*I have begun to understand why parents say no*
*why they can't share everything with their kids*
*But I now find myself in the same position*
*It's not very fun*
*But on this thought, I do not mull*
*lest I ruin it for everyone*

# 23. Curtains Down

*Staying up till 1 AM*
*laughing till our ribs break*
*then one person has to go*
*that doesn't mean the fun will end*
*one more person leaves*
*now it's just you and me*
*Several years pass*
*new faces enter,*
*they become old and exit*
*It's 3 in the morning again*
*I'm the only one left*
*I don't want to greet new faces anymore*
*It's time*
*I just want to take some rest*

# 24. Non-mutual Partings

*It starts with not talking to you as much*
*Then it goes to leaving you out*
*You share your secrets*
*and then they leave*
*They forget all about it*
*Sometimes, they are made to*
*but it stays with me*
*those memories have been plastered to my brain*
*All the ups*
*and the downs*
*Mutual memories shared as friends*
*now evaluated on the basis of future careers*
*They are now engraved in my mind, for now and forever*
*And then one day, they expect me to forgive them*
*After all the pain they've caused me*
*in*
*separation*
*is it really a forgivable cause?*

# 25. Being a Tween

*Being a tween is not that bad*
*These have been the best years of my life*
*Though it's full of highs and lows*
*these are the years when you make most memories*
*You make new friends, and you lose some*
*In these years you learn the most*
*Your personality changes and lets you know who you are*
*Maybe I over-exaggerated the situation a bit*
*But the lessons you learn when you're a tween*
*The moment you start doubting yourself over the advice given*
*and look for alternatives*
*know that you're neither in the right nor the wrong*
*but you've finally learnt to trust yourself*
*You may confide in others, your trust might be broken by them*
*But don't ever forget that voice of yours*
*that has now begun to speak*
*In times, when you feel alone in a family picture or in a crowd*
*when people fail to understand your words that have now*
*changed their tone*
*you will be anxious*
*but helpless no more*
*You'll have learnt to deal with it,*

ANIKA MALHOTRA

*in your own sweet way*

# Bio

Anika Malhotra is a 7$^{th}$ grader and an aspiring writer who is often asked questions befitting an adult. She spends most of her time playing video games and talking to her friends on Discord. She is a TV show and movie enthusiast. Some interests of hers include: listening to music, gaming, and discovering herself – not in that particular order.